OVER THE EDGE
A Kid's Guide To Niagara Falls, Ontario Canada

PHOTOGRAPHY BY JOHN D. WEIGAND
POETRY BY PENELOPE DYAN

Bellissima Publishing, LLC
Jamul, California
www.bellissimapublishing.com

Copyright © 2010 by Penny D. Weigand and John D. Weigand

All rights reserved. No part of this book may be
reproduced or transmitted in any form or by any means,
electronic or mechanical, including photocopying,
recording, or by any other means, or by any information or
storage retrieval system, without permission from the publisher.

ISBN 978-1-935630-07-4

First Edition

For Kids Who Love To Chase Rainbows,
And For Parents Who Love
To Chase Rainbows With Them!

Over The Edge
Bellissima Publishing, LLC

Introduction

Somewhere under the rainbow flowers grow, and maybe that is where you will find your pot of gold. Photographer John D. Weigand and author Penelope Dyan take you on another fun filled journey to Niagara falls, Ontario, Canada. See some of the fun stuff kids can do while they are there, and take some time to marvel at this creation of nature that has done its best to serve mankind in its very special way. Celebrate the glorious beauty of Niagara falls, where you are sure to find a rainbow!

The Niagara Falls are the great waterfalls of the Niagara River that are located between Ontario, Canada and New York, USA. Niagara Falls is separated into two main sections, the Canadian Horseshoe Falls, most of which is on the Canadian side, and the American Falls which is on the American side!

Niagara Falls formed when glaciers receded at the end of the Wisconsin glaciation (the last ice age). The water from the glaciers formed the Great Lakes, and the Great Lakes carved a path through the Niagara Escarpment as the water made its way to the Atlantic Ocean. The Niagara Falls are very wide, and are world known for their great beauty.

The Falls are a natural source of electric power, and this is probably why the Falls have so many rainbows! Electricity is the pot of gold everyone can surely find at the end of the Niagara Falls' rainbows!

If you are looking for a rainbow, Niagara Falls, Ontario, Canada is one place you can surely find one!

Over The Edge
Bellissima Publishing, LLC

Over The Edge
A Kid's Guide To Niagara Falls, Ontario Canada

Photography By John D. Weigand
Poetry By Penelope Dyan

If you are looking for a rainbow,
You could take a boat.

or take The Falls' Incline Rail. . .

or walk from here to there. . .
A rainbow could be just anywhere!

As you gaze at the USA
(and at American Falls)
you will ask yourself where they will be---
those famous rainbows you came to see?

You don't see them at the Horseshoe Falls
as you stop and stare.
In fact, all you see is water!
There's water everywhere!

But you do see some Canadian bears
as you go walking on your way.
And a Canadian flag hangs above the shelves
where those sweet teddies stay!

And while you haven't found a rainbow
(so far) at the either of the Niagara Falls,
You did see a great big. . . big, big bunch
Of very cute Canadian dolls!

You CAN buy a REALLY good
Canadian hot dog to eat!

You can go to a wax museum
for another special treat!

Or you can eat candy and chocolates galore,
If you take your parents to THIS candy store!

And you could ALWAYS (as a last resort) put on a raincoat and take a boat!

And then you'll see it, straight ahead,
A beautiful rainbow, blue, yellow, and red!

And under the rainbow you will float, smiling, and wet on that little boat!

And later you can go up really high,
on a ferris wheel that touches the sky.

You can go to a place lit colorfully bright and play lots of fun games until it is night!

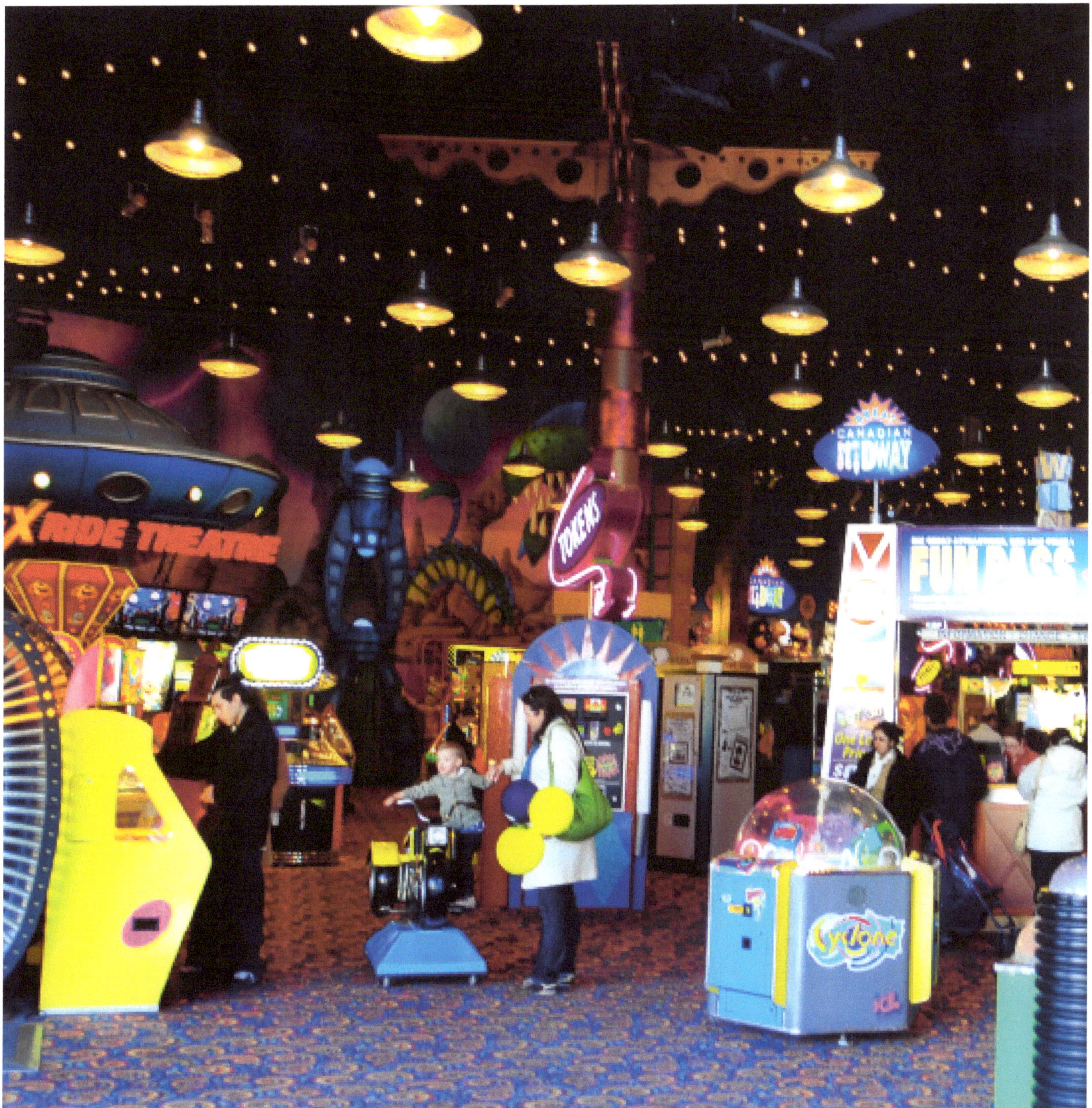
RIDE THEATRE
TOKENS
CANADIAN
MIDWAY
FUN PASS
Cyclone

You can buy a wacky hat to wear,
the kind that make people stop and stare.

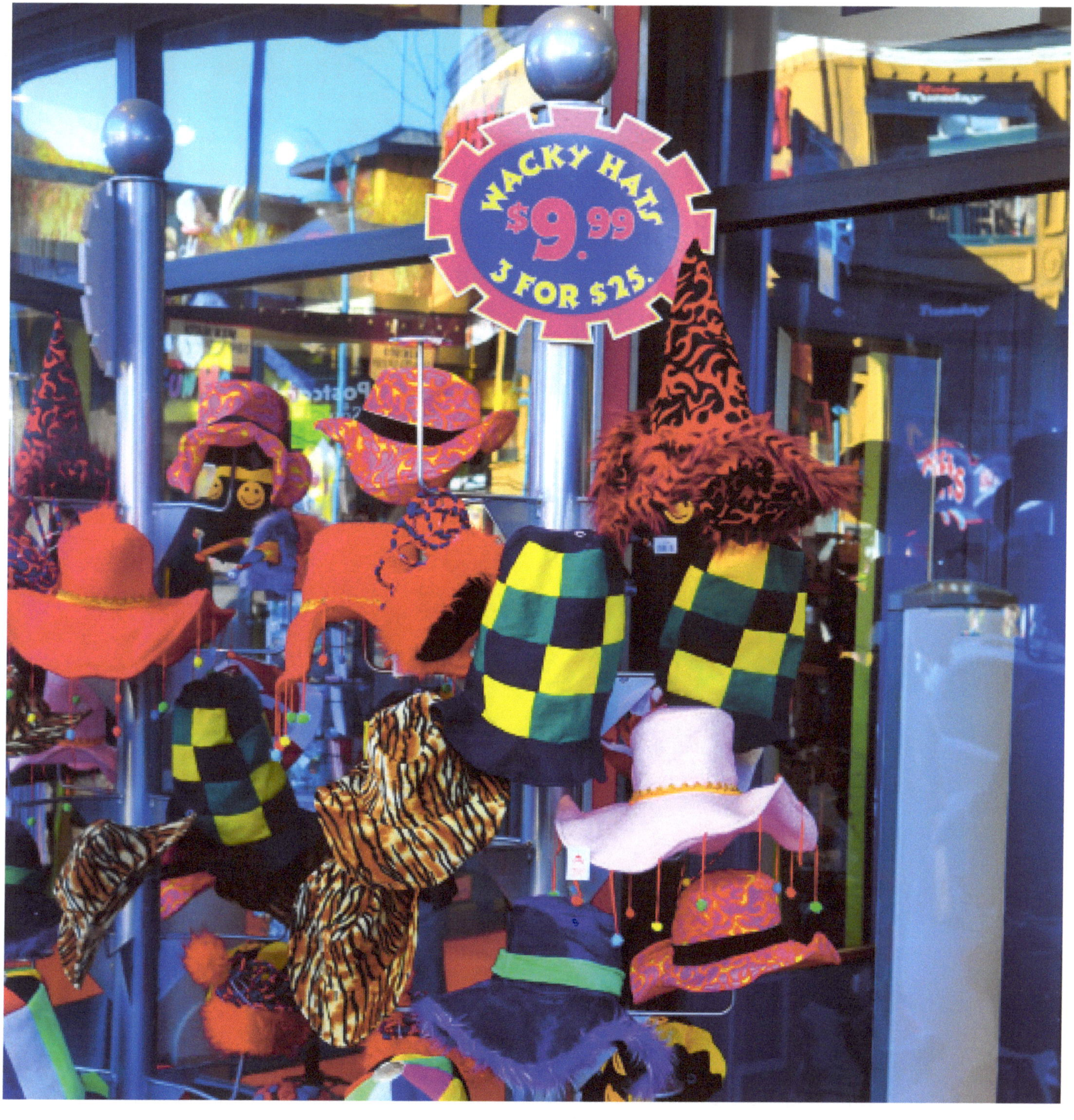
WACKY HATS
$9.99
3 FOR $25.

When the sun goes down
and they make the falls blue,
you will think they did it,
just for you.
And in a way they REALLY did!
BECAUSE it's ALWAYS fun to please a kid!

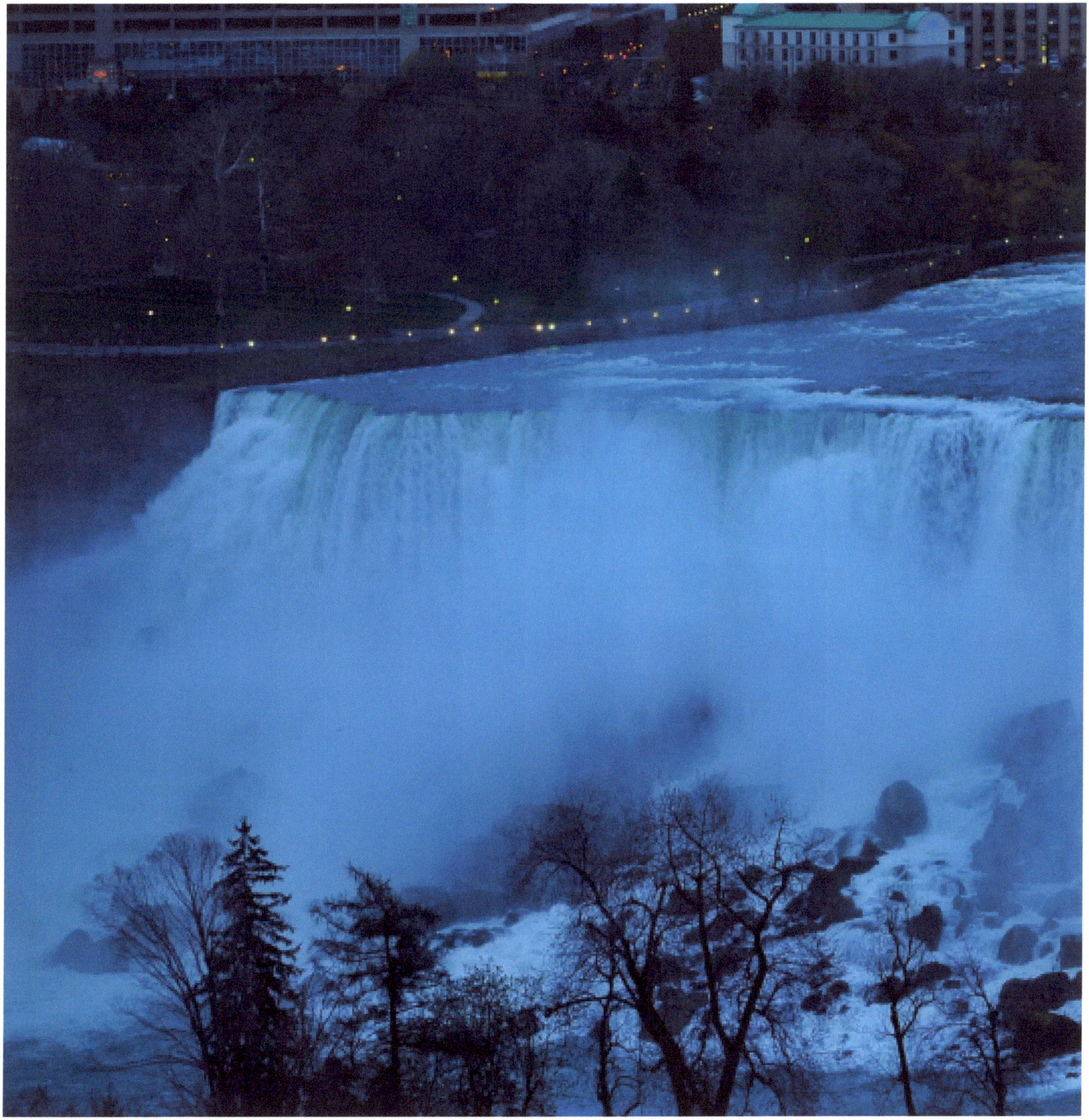

And when the Falls turn yellow and red,
your mom will say, "It's time for bed."
In your hotel she will tuck you
under the covers for the night,
and then you will sleep 'till morning's light.

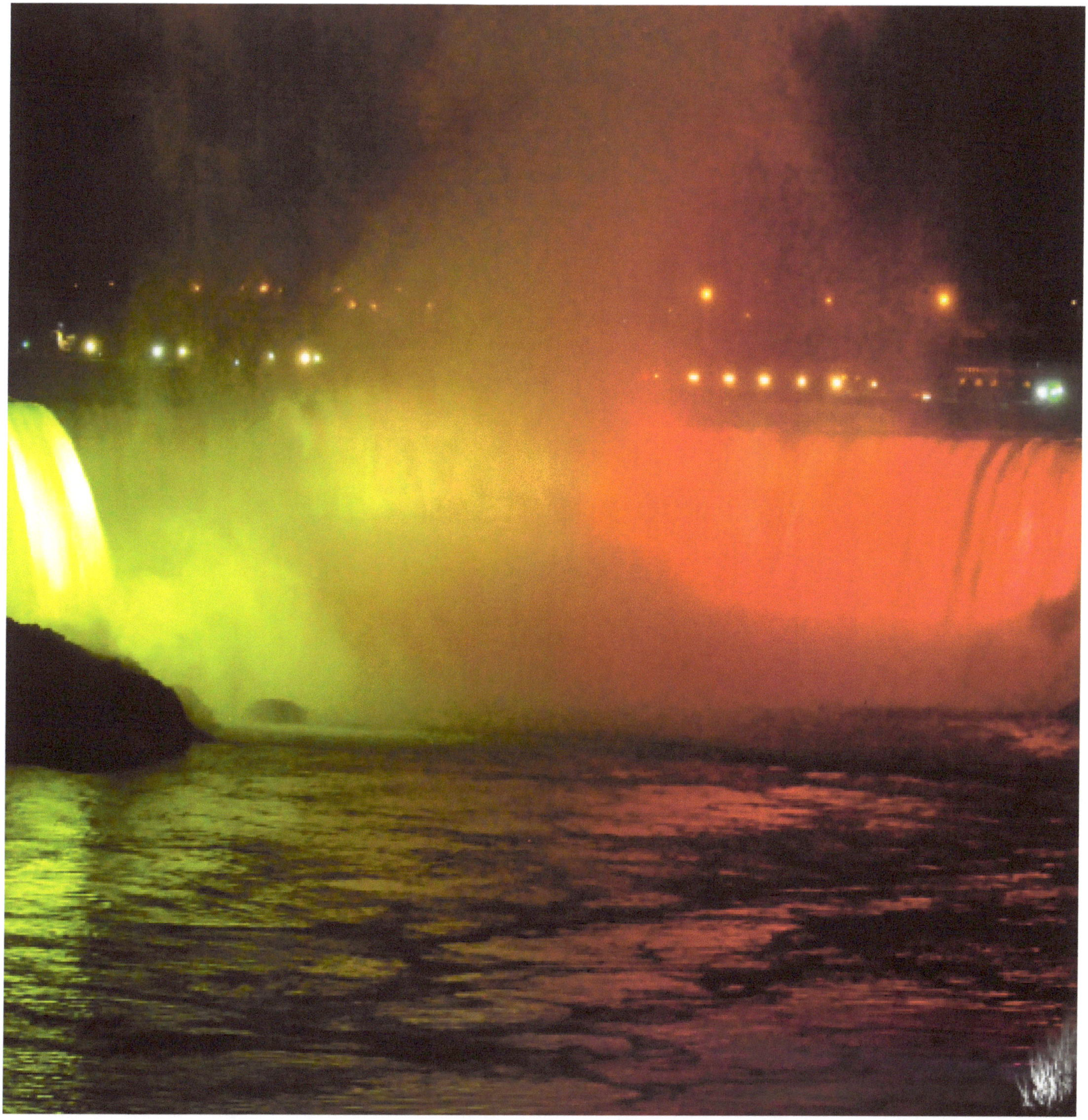

And in the morning you will see,
another rainbow, maybe two or three.
You will wonder where it is
(as you have been told)
that those leprechauns are
with those pots of gold?
You can't travel to the rainbow's end.
It's way too far around the bend.
But you CAN bask in its promise,
right where you are;
and you CAN make a wish upon a star!
You CAN make your dreams come true.
And just HOW you do it, is up to YOU!

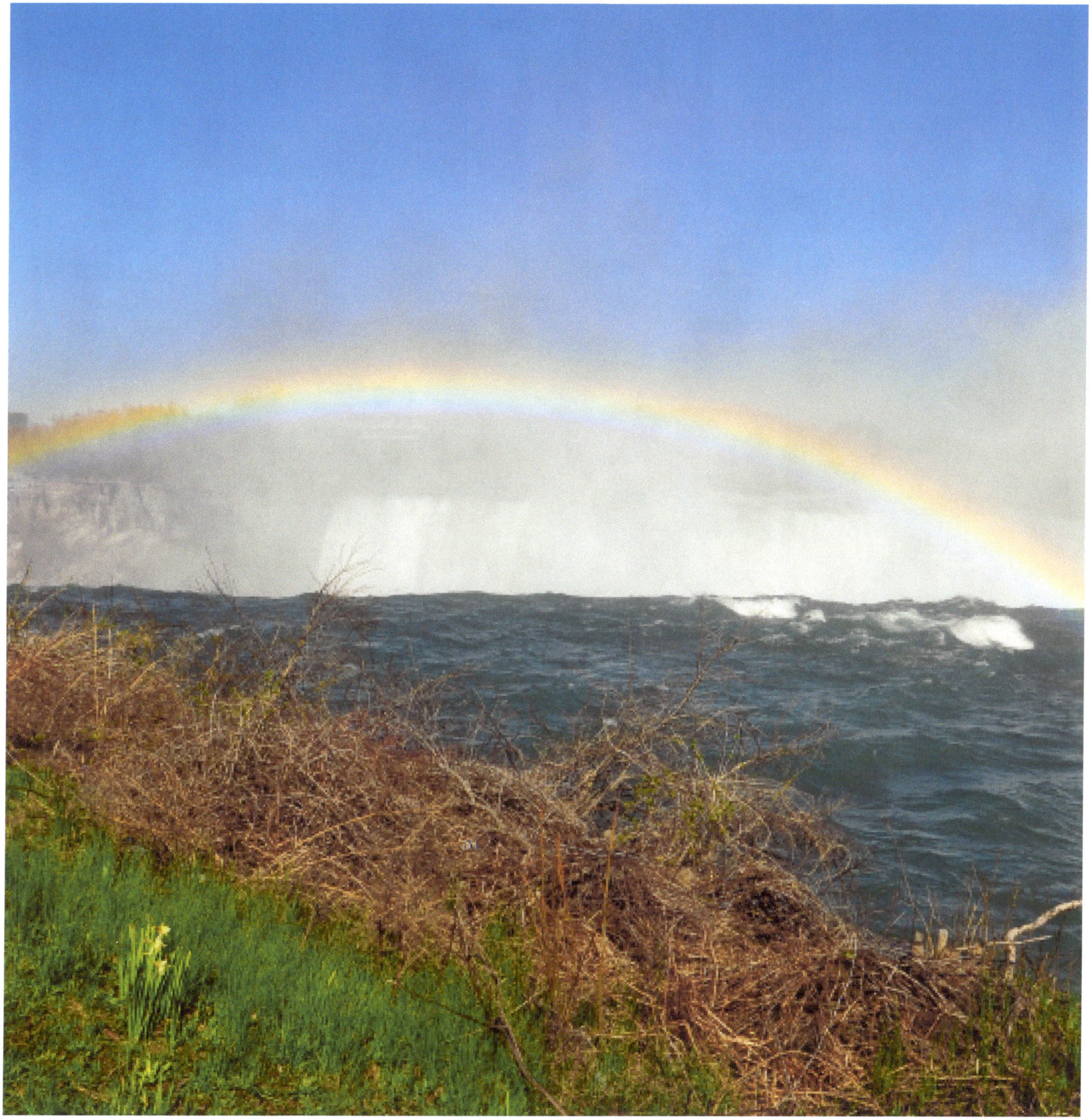

The End

Whenever you get a chance, reach out and touch a rainbow!

CPSIA information can be obtained
at www.ICGtesting.com
Printed in the USA
LVHW050142091219
639857LV00014B/776/P